COLOSSIANS

BEING LIKE JESUS

Other studies in the Not Your Average Bible Study series

For updates on this series, visit lexhampress.com/nyab

COLOSSIANS

BEING LIKE JESUS

NOT YOUR AVERAGE BIBLE STUDY

JOHN D. BARRY

Colossians: Being Like Jesus
Not Your Average Bible Study

Copyright 2014 Lexham Press
Adapted with permission from content originally published in *Bible Study Magazine* (Issues 2.4–3.3)

Lexham Press, 1313 Commercial St., Bellingham, WA 98225
LexhamPress.com

ISBN 978-1-57-799547-0

Assistant Editors: Jessi Strong, Elizabeth Vince, Joel Wilcox
Cover Design: Christine Gerhart
Typesetting: ProjectLuz.com

CONTENTS

HOW TO USE THIS RESOURCE

Not Your Average Bible Study is a series of in-depth Bible studies that can be used for individual or group study. Depending on your individual needs or your group pace, you may opt to cover one lesson a week or more.

Each lesson prompts you to dig deep into the Word—as such, we recommend you use your preferred translation with this study. The author used his own translation, but included quotations from the English Standard Version. Whatever Bible version you use, please be sure you leave ample time to get into the Bible itself.

To assist you, we recommend using the Faithlife Study Bible, which is also edited by John D. Barry. You can download this digital resource for free for your tablet, phone, personal computer, or use it online. Go to FaithlifeBible.com to learn more.

May God bless you in the study of His Word.

INTRODUCTION

"I rejoice in my sufferings for your sake."

Paul spoke these words to a scribe, likely while in a dark pit, chained to a guard. Pain, filth, turmoil *and rejoicing*? Most of us would be saying, "God, why have you abandoned me?" Not Paul—he saw an opportunity to serve Jesus.

Paul met Christ on his way to kill Christians. Via a blinding light, scales on his eyes, and a vision, he became a Christ-follower. But it wasn't Paul's vision that gave him spiritual stamina. His fellow workers in the early church seemed to be enduring similar circumstances (Col 4:10-17). It was his dependence on a God, who could overcome not only the visible forces of evil, but also the unseen forces that lurked in the darkness.

COLOSSIANS 1:1–14

While in prison in Rome, Paul had a scribe write down a message to the Colossians (compare 4:18). The scribe then gave the letter to Tychicus and a runaway slave named Onesimus to deliver to the churches at Colossae and Laodicea (4:7–9). They also carried a second, personal letter requesting that Philemon, a leader in the church and the owner of Onesimus, free the fugitive slave.

The beginning of Colossians (1:1–2:5) tells us how we can be like Christ. We learn the theology necessary to fight evil and the practicality of loving Jesus. The focus of the first section of the letter is Paul's identity, why we should be thankful, and the need for prayer (1:1–14). Suffering is a battle for our souls, and Christ can be the victor.

Christ is at the center of Paul's letter, and the focal point of every issue he addresses. Colossians tells us how we can make Christ the center of our lives too. Our first eight studies will teach us what it means to join Christ in His victory over darkness.

TASTE-TESTING COLOSSIANS

Pray that God would reveal the message of Colossians to you.

Read all of Colossians aloud in one sitting.

This letter was meant to be read out loud, so we need to hear it before we can interpret it (4:16). (Double underline transition words like "now," "therefore," "yet" and "but," as well as negations like "no" and "not.")

Read all the verses again where these transition words are used. Write a short summary of each of these verses. What do these verses tell you about the general gist of the letter?

_____

_____

_____

_____

_____

_____

_____

Now we have taste-tested Colossians—had a bit of an appetizer. But to get to the main course, we need to pray. The late scholar Brevard Childs once said, "Herein lies the secret of biblical interpretation: Wherever the Spirit is not present, there is no great explanation possible." If you want to understand Paul's letter, if you want to hear God, listen to the Spirit. Move Christ to the center of all you do.

THE MAIN COURSE

Pray that God would strengthen you through Christ and the Spirit.

Read all of Colossians aloud in one sitting.

Reading the entire letter will allow you to see how the ideas Paul develops later in the letter are based on what he says at the beginning. (Draw square brackets or a box around the words "first," "new," "light," "alive" and "hidden.")

Read aloud each of the lines with key words in them. Who is at the center of Paul's theology? (Who is he writing about?) Use four adjectives (description words) to lay out how Paul understands this character. How should Paul's understanding of this character shape the way we look at the world?

_____

_____

_____

_____

_____

Name some important events that have changed the world. How do these events affect our lives?

_____

_____

_____

_____

_____

Last week, we taste-tested Colossians. Now we are getting to the main course: we're going to understand Paul's theology. When we combine study with prayer, we get an incredible result: theology shaped by our experiences—an understanding of God that is based (in part) on contemplation, prayer and practice. At the center of Colossians is the idea that our understanding of Christ directly reflects how we live. If we don't understand Him, we can't live like Him. Being like Christ means finding Christ everywhere—in all parts of life. Seeing Him in everything is a constant reminder that we need to show Him to others.

COLOSSIANS IS ABOUT CHRIST— AND OUR ACTIONS IN HIM

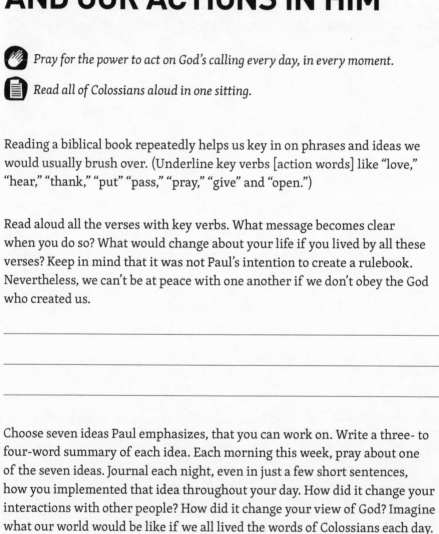

Pray for the power to act on God's calling every day, in every moment.

Read all of Colossians aloud in one sitting.

Reading a biblical book repeatedly helps us key in on phrases and ideas we would usually brush over. (Underline key verbs [action words] like "love," "hear," "thank," "put" "pass," "pray," "give" and "open.")

Read aloud all the verses with key verbs. What message becomes clear when you do so? What would change about your life if you lived by all these verses? Keep in mind that it was not Paul's intention to create a rulebook. Nevertheless, we can't be at peace with one another if we don't obey the God who created us.

_____

_____

_____

Choose seven ideas Paul emphasizes, that you can work on. Write a three- to four-word summary of each idea. Each morning this week, pray about one of the seven ideas. Journal each night, even in just a few short sentences, how you implemented that idea throughout your day. How did it change your interactions with other people? How did it change your view of God? Imagine what our world would be like if we all lived the words of Colossians each day.

_____

_____

_____

ADDING "SAINT" TO YOUR RÉSUMÉ

Pray that Christ would show you what it means to be a saint.

Read Colossians 1:1–2:5. Reflect on verses 1:1–2.

Paul calls himself an "apostle." The apostles were Christ's ambassadors. They carried out His ministry and teachings. But who is Paul an apostle of? How did he become an apostle? (Think about what Colossians says first, and then read Acts 8:1–25 and Acts 9:1–22.)

_____

_____

_____

_____

_____

With whom is Paul writing his letter (Col 1:1)? Look up this individual in a concordance or in Bible software. What did you learn about him?

_____

_____

_____

_____

Who is Paul's letter addressed to? Colossians 1:2 talks about "saints." "Saint" is a status given to you when you believe in Christ, not a status to be earned. It means "holy one." All who believe in Christ have been made holy in His eyes. So, as Mark Driscoll once said, go add "Saint" to your business card and résumé.

What are the two things Paul wishes for the church at Colossae (Col 1:2)?

_____

_____

_____

The title of "saint" has been given to you freely through Christ's grace. You can have peace through the Holy Spirit. How does this change your perspective? Since you are constantly representing Christ as His saint, how should your interactions with other people change?

_____

_____

_____

_____

FROM SLAVE TO BROTHER

Pray that the Spirit would help you give thanks—even in trials.

Read Colossians 1:1–2:5. Reflect on verse 1:3–8.

For whom is Paul thankful (Col 1:2–3)? *Who* does Paul thank? *When* is Paul thankful? *Why* is Paul thankful (Col 1:4–5)?

_____

_____

_____

_____

What have the Colossians "heard about beforehand" (Col 1:5)? What "has come" to the Colossians (Col 1:6)? What is "bearing fruit and increasing"?

_____

_____

_____

_____

What do we learn about the Colossians' relationship with God at the end of Colossians 1:6? This tells us what type of people Paul is addressing.

_____

_____

_____

_____

Who ministered to the Colossians and told Paul about them (1:7–8)? Did Paul personally know the Colossians, or does he know them only by word of mouth? Before drawing a conclusion, read the book of Philemon (especially verses 5 and 19).

_____

_____

_____

_____

Remember, Philemon was part of the house church the letter to the Colossians was sent to; he was likely the host. Paul was not only elderly and imprisoned for his belief in Christ when he wrote the letter to Philemon; he was also in a difficult position: arguing for a close friend's freedom from indentured slavery. Why was he so bold?

_____

_____

_____

_____

Christ has freed all of us. Paul was fighting a spiritual battle on all fronts, but he gave thanks in everything. Giving thanks is the cure to bitterness, and more often than not, depression. What can you be thankful for today? How could thankfulness change your outlook?

_____

_____

_____

_____

"I HAVE IT UNDER CONTROL"

Pray that the Spirit would reveal God's will for your life.

Read Colossians 1:1–2:5. Reflect on verse 1:9.

In Colossians 1:9, Paul turns his focus from thanksgiving to prayer. Prayer is a natural result of thanksgiving—thankfulness makes us stop focusing on ourselves and start focusing on God. What does Paul ask God for on behalf of the Colossians (1:9)? How can you be "filled with the knowledge of [God's] will in all wisdom and spiritual insight"? (Read Jam 1:5–8 and 3:13–18.)

_____

_____

_____

_____

Why do you need God's wisdom? What areas of your life currently require godly discernment?

_____

_____

_____

_____

What do you need to give up for Christ to be the center of *these areas* of your life—for Christ to take control?

_____

_____

_____

SEPARATION ANXIETY— SEPARATED FROM CHRIST, SEPARATED FROM JOY

Pray that God would teach you to "walk" like Christ.

Read Colossians 1:1–14. Reflect on verses 1:10–12.

What type of "walk" does God require of us (1:10)? What does it mean to "bear fruit"? (Read Gal 5:16–26 and Psa 1.)

_____

_____

_____

_____

Colossians 1:11 echoes Galatians 5:16–26. Which "fruit" is mentioned in both books? Why does Paul highlight these attributes?

_____

_____

_____

_____

Many times we think of "walking with Christ" as hard work, and it can be. But we are called to walk with Christ *"with joy"* (1:11). Someone who is joyful is optimistic about life because of what Christ has done for them, despite their circumstances (like Paul in prison). Do you exude joy? Colossians 1:12 tells you how to have joy. Living "with joy" is tied to Christ's ability to strengthen us "with all power" (Col 1:11). Once again, Christ is the center.

In what activities do you struggle to have joy? Work? Family? Friends? Church? How can more joy be brought to these areas of your life? How can Christ dwell in these activities?

_____

_____

_____

_____

FROM DARKNESS TO LIGHT

Pray that Christ would show you what it means to be redeemed.

Read Colossians 1:1–14. Reflect on verses 1:13–14.

Who is the "he" in 1:13? Is it Jesus? The Father? Both? Before drawing any conclusions, think about the larger context of Colossians 1, and what it says about Christ's relationship to God the Father.

_____

_____

_____

_____

What areas of your life currently belong to the domain of darkness? Are you willing to let Christ's "light" shine in them? Who do you know that can help you overcome the darkness? Reach out to God, and reach out to them.

_____

_____

_____

_____

Spend the rest of the time you would usually spend studying Colossians to pray about ways God can help you overcome darkness in your life.

_____

_____

_____

_____

CONCLUSION

God has shined His "light" in the "domain of darkness." His light is Christ. He has moved us from where darkness reigns to where *He* reigns. The shadows will tremble. Darkness will try to hide. "The image of the invisible God" came to earth so that we can *visibly be like Jesus*. No matter what pain, turmoil, or darkness you are flailing against, Christ can intervene. Christ can be victor in your life because He is already victorious over the earth and all powers. May His power reign in your life, and may the Holy Spirit work in you so that you can be like Jesus.

COLOSSIANS 1:15–23

1. Present with God and creation from the beginning—*firstborn of creation.*
2. Made peace between God and humanity by overcoming death—*firstborn from the dead.* 3. Unified broken people with each other and with creation—*first in the church (the head).* 4. Declares us holy and blameless before God—*first to fully reconcile us with God.*

When Paul wrote to the Colossians from prison in Rome, He told them to make Christ the center. By nature of His unique position as the firstborn of creation, Jesus connects everything: us to each other, us to creation, and (most importantly) us to God. He brings the broken pieces of our fallen world together again. Paul explains who Christ is in an elegant song of praise in Colossians 1:15–23. In the next eight studies, we will learn what it means for Christ to be the firstborn of creation and the firstborn of the resurrection, how we are redeemed through Him, and why we are without excuse when we don't believe.

GOD'S SON IS UNIQUE

✋ *Pray that God would show you what it means for Christ to reign in your life.*

📄 *Read all of Colossians aloud in one sitting. Reflect on verse 1:15.*

What does it mean for Jesus to be the "image" of the invisible God (Col 1:15)? Think about how Adam and Eve were meant to be the "image" of God—as people who brought order to chaos (Gen 1:27-28)? Does bearing God's "image" have to do with actions, a status, or both?

_____

_____

_____

_____

_____

When Paul says that Christ was the "firstborn" of creation in Colossians 1:15, he is making two points:

1.   Jesus is the first eternal, spiritual being made flesh and born as a human

2.   Jesus is the head of all of creation—the one in charge.

If Christ is in charge of creation and holds a unique position, what is there to fear? How would your life look different if you fully embraced Christ as the one in charge of your life?

_____

_____

_____

_____

How would the lives of those around you be affected if you demonstrated every day that someone greater than yourself has the ability to rule your life and this world?

_____

_____

_____

_____

ALL THINGS GREAT AND SMALL

Pray that you would be open to letting God demonstrate His love for His creation through you.

Read all of Colossians aloud in one sitting. Reflect on verse 1:16.

Repetitively hearing something makes it memorable. Coaches and music instructors say that any given range of motion has to be done around 100 times, exactly the same, for your muscles to memorize it. When an athlete or musician is under pressure, their muscle memory takes over—it overcomes their mind. When we are under stress or are anxious, we need God's Spirit to take over. Reading the text repetitively helps us to prepare. It engages our spiritual memory.

What was created *through* Christ (Col 1:16)? What was created *for* Him? Does anything have control *over* Him? And by extension, can anything rule *over* those who have been freed *by* Him?

_____

_____

_____

_____

_____

_____

_____

_____

Colossians 1:16 tells us that "all things were created through [God's Son] and for him." Creation—whether good or bad—was created for Christ to lovingly rule over. This recalls the witty book, *All Creatures Great and Small*, where James Herriot teaches us how to love (and laugh at) God's creation, no matter how dirty it is. Since creation was made for Jesus, He must (at times) find irony in watching us and His other creatures make a muck of things—He no doubt knows better than we do. And it's because of His love for us that He came to this ironic, mixed-up world that often hates the very God that created it.

How would our world look different if we loved what Jesus does—all things great and small? How could you improve your relationship with God's creation and other people?

_____

_____

_____

_____

_____

CHRIST AT THE CENTER

Pray that God would show you how you can better center your life on Him.

Read all of Colossians aloud in one sitting. Reflect on verses 1:17 and the first part of 1:18.

What does it mean for God's Son to be "before all things" (Col 1:17)? (Think about this in light of Col 1:15–16.) Is verse 1:17 referring to when Christ came to be, or His position of authority, or both?

_____

_____

_____

_____

What is "held together" in Christ (Col 1:17)? What are we connected to because of our connection to Him?

_____

_____

_____

Colossians 1:15–18 tells us that Christ is in charge of all creation, including the church. As a member of Christ's "body"—the community of believers—how can you be more diligent about showing that He is in charge?

_____

_____

_____

_____

Is Christ the center in your Christian community, or is a person or group of people its center? If Christ isn't at the center, what needs to change? And how can you graciously help move your congregation in a new direction? Remember, church is not limited to a building; it is a group of people.

_____

_____

_____

_____

FIRSTBORN FROM THE DEAD

Pray that God would reveal to you what it means for Christ to bring you reconciliation.

Read Colossians 1:1–2:5. Reflect on the second part of verse 1:18.

Colossians 1:18 says that Jesus is "the firstborn from the dead." Use a Bible dictionary or Bible software to look up "firstborn." This word in verse 1:18 is about Jesus' rank—His special status. He is the only resurrected person who guarantees new life to those who follow Him. This is the basis for Paul's message that Christ "holds together" everything. He reconciles us to God, each other and creation. Christ being "preeminent" means something similar: He is the one in charge—He deserves the highest dignity and honor.

Christ's resurrection brings us reconciliation with God: back into a relationship with Him. What patterns do you need to alter in light of this?

_____

_____

_____

_____

_____

_____

LESSON 5

GOD DWELLING WITH US

👐 *Pray that God would reveal to you how He dwelled in Christ, and subsequently can dwell in you.*

📄 *Read Colossians 1:1–2:5. Reflect on verses 1:19–20.*

Colossians 1:19–20 concludes what Paul said in Colossians 1:18. What does it mean for "the fullness of God to dwell" in Jesus (Col 1:19)? What was reconciled to God through Jesus (Col 1:20)?

_____

_____

_____

_____

How did Jesus make peace (Col 1:20)?

_____

_____

_____

_____

Read Hebrews 9:11–15. What light does the author of Hebrews shed on Paul's words in Colossians?

_____

_____

_____

_____

Jesus, as the fullness of God in a human body, died a bloody death for us—so that we could be reconciled to God. In being reconciled to Him, the fullness of God can dwell in us via the Holy Spirit. Are you embracing the fullness of God? What needs to change about your life for you to be free in Christ—for you to embrace the reconciliation He has brought you?

_____

_____

_____

_____

GOD REVEALED

Pray that God would show you how He has revealed Himself to all people.

Read Colossians 1:1–2:5. Reflect on verses 1:21–23.

In Colossians 1:21, Paul describes the previous state of those in the Colossian church. Were you once in the same state? Are you still there? What does Colossians tell us about breaking free from that state?

_____

_____

_____

_____

Colossians 1:22 tells us precisely how Christ reconciled us. What are the events it describes (1:22)? Why did Christ reconcile us to God?

_____

_____

_____

Now that Christ has reconciled us, what are we called to do (1:23)?

_____

_____

_____

_____

When he speaks of staying "attached" to "the hope of the gospel," Paul is not making a statement about how we stay reconciled to Christ, because reconciliation is Christ's work, not ours. Rather, he is speaking about how we keep up communication with God, and grow our relationship with Him.

How has the gospel been proclaimed (1:23)? Read Romans 1:19-20. How does God reveal Himself? How does your perception of the ways God reveals Himself need to change? How will this change your daily interactions with other people?

_____

_____

_____

_____

CHRIST BEFORE EVERYTHING

Pray that God would help you reset your priorities.

Read Colossians 1:1–2:5 aloud. Reflect on verses 1:15–23.

Now read Genesis 1. How is what Paul says about Jesus connected to what God does in Genesis 1? What is the first way God revealed Himself to people? What is His first commandment?

_____

_____

_____

Read John 1:1–5 and 1:9–18. Both Genesis and John tell us about "the beginning" and both assume that God was present in the beginning. But what are the differences between Genesis 1 and John 1? How does Colossians further elaborate upon this?

_____

_____

_____

Read Hebrews 1:1–4. It is similar to Colossians 1. The author of Hebrews explains that God's Son has always been present, and thus should define every moment of our lives. Why would each of these authors trace Jesus to the creation events? What is so significant about Christ's involvement in them?

_____

_____

_____

_____

How do these passages shape our understanding of Christ's place in the world and in our lives?

_____

_____

_____

_____

How does a view of God, based on these passages, modify the way you approach your daily walk with God?

_____

_____

_____

_____

GOD'S SON— HIGHEST PRIORITY

Pray that God would make you open to change so that you can be more like Jesus.

Read Colossians 1:1–2:5 aloud.

Colossians emphasizes that Christ should be at the center of our lives. Take a moment to evaluate whether Christ is at the center of yours. Think about your priorities—not just what you think they are, but what they *really* are. How can you reprioritize your life to make your relationship with Jesus the highest priority?

_____

_____

_____

_____

The only way you can be like Jesus is to spend time with Him. Spending time with God doesn't just mean prayer, as important as that is. It means trying to glorify God through how you treat other people, all the time. It means making God's priorities your priorities. Take the rest of the time you would usually spend studying Colossians to pray about the changes God has convicted you to make through your study of Colossians 1:1–2:5. What is He teaching you?

_____

_____

_____

_____

_____

CONCLUSION

When Jesus is at the center of our lives, our perspective on the world is altered: Pain seems bearable and peculiar circumstances don't seem pointless. That's precisely why Paul could be in a dark pit, chained to a Roman guard, and still say, "I rejoice in my sufferings" (Col 1:24). Paul knew that through his sufferings, he could help the church become more like Jesus. Every moment is a chance to be more like Jesus—to perceive how He is working in our world. May you move Him to the center of all that you do.

COLOSSIANS 1:24–2:7

Reading Paul's letters is like drinking bold, black coffee. When we realize that Paul is drinking a much stronger blend of spirituality, our spirits wake up. But Paul's boldness can also be disconcerting: "I fill up in my flesh what is lacking of the afflictions of Christ, on behalf of his body which is the church" (Col 1:24). It sounds like Paul is audaciously saying, "Christ didn't suffer enough, and the Church certainly isn't enduring enough pain. So I'm glad I can help meet the quota." Paul is bold, but not that bold—nor that misguided.

In Colossians 1:24, Paul is explaining that his imprisonment in Rome is a way for the church to be "filled up." When we are persecuted, the cup isn't half empty; it's half full. Paul is emphasizing just how ironic it is that Christ, the ultimate sufferer, can use tragic circumstances to manifest His presence.

Most of us are still learning to see suffering as an opportunity for Christ to live through us. And we certainly have much to learn about being a diligent Christ-follower. But what we can glean from Paul can made a big difference.

Even though we would never wish for pain, it can help us identify with Jesus. For Paul, suffering was an opportunity to edify the body, the church. This seems like a frustrating theological stance. Yet Paul explains why it is empowering. In the next eight studies, we will learn what Paul means. We will learn how we can rejoice in our suffering, be strengthened by God, and have enduring faith.

THE IRONY OF REJOICING IN SUFFERING

🤚 *Pray that God would help you rejoice in suffering.*

📄 *Read Colossians 1:1–2:6 aloud. Reflect on verse 1:24.*

Why does Paul rejoice in his sufferings? For whom does he suffer?

_____

_____

_____

_____

When Paul talks about "what is lacking in Christ's afflictions," he is not suggesting that Christ's suffering is not sufficient for salvation or reconciliation with God. Instead, he is suggesting that Christ's mission to suffer for (and alongside) His people did not end with His death—it is carried forward by His apostles, like Paul. In 2 Corinthians 12:9, Paul cites Jesus as saying, "My grace is sufficient for you, for my power is made perfect in weakness." Paul then says, "Therefore I will boast all the more gladly of my weaknesses, so that the power of Christ may rest upon me. For the sake of Christ, then, I am content with weaknesses, insults, hardships, persecutions, and calamities. For when I am weak, then I am strong" (2 Cor 12:9–10 ESV). *For what* was Paul suffering? *Why* was he suffering?

_____

_____

_____

_____

We are commanded to rejoice in our sufferings (1 Pet 4:12–19). Can you say legitimately that you rejoice in your sufferings? If not, what needs to change about your life for you to make that statement?

_____

_____

_____

_____

STEWARDS, NOT RULERS

Pray that the Spirit would reveal to you areas of your life you need to steward, not control.

Read Colossians 1:1–29 aloud. Reflect on verses 1:24–25.

Why does Paul expect his suffering to help the church? (Think about this in light of 2 Cor 12:9–10.)

_____

_____

_____

_____

Why does Paul call the church "the body" (Col 1:24)? What imagery is he trying to evoke? (Consider what Paul says about Christ's afflictions in 1:15–23.)

_____

_____

_____

_____

Read Romans 7:4–6 and 8:9–11. How does reflecting on this passage change the way you interpret Colossians 1:24?

_____

_____

_____

_____

Of what did Paul become a minister (1:25)? Paul uses the term "stewardship from God" to define his role—meaning that God has given him groups of people to lead, but that his ministry (and the people involved) belong to God. Why do you think he chooses this term? What are you a "steward" of? What should you stop trying to control?

_____

_____

_____

_____

How does Paul define his vocation? What is his primary duty (1:25)? Should we make this our primary duty as well?

_____

_____

_____

_____

Paul, like most of us, also had a regular job (making tents), yet he understood his primary duty to be something other than tent making. In what ways can you be a minister in everyday life? How can you proclaim the gospel through your actions?

_____

_____

_____

_____

MYSTERY

✋ *Pray that Christ would help you understand His mystery and join Him in the journey to reveal it.*

📄 *Read Colossians 1:15–29. Reflect on verses 1:25–26.*

What "word of God" is Paul referencing: the Old Testament, what Jesus said, or both? (Remember: Paul met Jesus in a vision, but never knew Jesus before His death and resurrection.)

_____

_____

_____

What "mystery" was "hidden for ages and generations" (1:26)? Where was this "mystery" hidden? (Think about this in terms of the "word of God" Paul references.)

_____

_____

_____

_____

How has the "mystery" been revealed? Read Luke 24:13–27. How is the "word of God" and the mystery of Jesus revealed to the two men on the road?

_____

_____

_____

_____

How can you join God in revealing His mystery to other people? What can you do tomorrow and throughout your week that would help other people understand the mystery of Christ?

_____

_____

_____

_____

JESUS AMONG US

Pray that Christ would show you how He is present among us.

Read Colossians 1:22–29. Reflect on verse 1:27.

God has revealed the mystery of Christ to His saints (those who follow Jesus) (1:26). What did God "make known" (1:27)? Prior to Paul's ministry, the Jews—Christ-followers or not—had separated themselves from the Gentiles (non-Jews) in order to stay pure. Christ made Jews and Gentiles equal.

_____

_____

_____

_____

Read Acts 15:1–35. In light of this, what is so significant about what Paul says in Colossians 1:27?

_____

_____

_____

_____

How is "the riches of the glory" (that is, Christ) revealed? What is "the hope of glory" (1:27)?

_____

_____

_____

_____

Read John 17:20-21. How does having Christ "in us" change our lives? What changes do you need to make to better reflect Jesus to others?

_____

_____

_____

_____

EMPOWERMENT

Pray that the Spirit would show you how He can energize and empower you.

Read Colossians 1:22–2:7. Reflect on verses 1:28–29.

What do the "saints" (the "we" in the sentence) proclaim (1:28)?

_____

_____

_____

_____

_____

Why should we warn and teach everyone (1:28)? (Read Col 1:21–23.)

_____

_____

_____

_____

How do you think "maturity in Christ" should manifest itself in our lives (1:28)?

_____

_____

_____

_____

_____

Paul says that he discovers Christ's energy in his struggles, and lets Christ work powerfully within him (1:29). We seek empowerment, the will to overcome adversity, and energy in all sorts of places. How often do you seek it in Christ? How can you be more proactive in seeking Christ? What needs to change about your life for Christ to become the source of your energy and empowerment?

_____

_____

_____

_____

MISPLACED TREASURE

Pray that God would reveal to you what you need to reprioritize in your life.

Read Colossians 1:24–2:7. Reflect on verses 2:1–3.

Why does Paul want the Colossians and the Laodiceans (other believers who would have received this letter) to know "how great a struggle" he has endured (Col 2:1)? Have all the church members in Colossae and Laodicea met Paul?

_____

_____

_____

_____

_____

In what ways do Paul's struggles strengthen his message?

_____

_____

_____

_____

What is Paul's wish and prayer for the people the letter is addressed to (2:2)?

_____

_____

_____

_____

How do "the riches of full assurance of understanding and the knowledge of God's mystery" relate to what Paul said in Colossians 1:15–29? What do "love" and unity have to do with living out the "mystery" of Christ's calling on our lives?

_____

_____

_____

_____

We often misplace our values by focusing on treasures that are not of God. How do you need to reprioritize your values to center them on Christ—to place your treasures in what He offers (2:3)?

_____

_____

_____

_____

FIRM FAITH

Pray that Christ would teach you the essentials of having a firm faith.

Read Colossians 1:24–2:7. Reflect on verses 2:4–5.

Reread Colossians 1:24–2:3. What does Paul say so that the Colossians and Laodiceans will not be misled (Col 2:4)? Why does he say it?

_____

_____

_____

_____

Why is Paul rejoicing (2:5)? When Paul talks about the "good order" of the Colossian and Laodicean communities, he is referencing what he said in Colossians 1:3–8. What is so "good" about their "order"? What is their "order"?

_____

_____

_____

_____

Does having "firm faith" have to do with our ability to achieve something, or with God's ability to work through us? Think about this in light of what Paul says throughout Colossians 1:15–23 about Christ's role in the world.

_____

_____

_____

_____

Paul has firm faith through his suffering. How can you have faith like Paul? What are four practical steps you can take toward being more faithful to Christ? Write down the steps you come up with—then pray about them, and work on them throughout your week. Consider sharing your steps with another Christ-follower so they can hold you accountable.

_____

_____

_____

_____

ROOTED

Pray that Jesus would teach you how to better root your life in Him.

Read Colossians 1:24–2:7. Reflect on verses 2:6–7.

Colossians 2:6–7 is the conclusion of what Paul has said in 1:15–2:5. What does Paul ask us to do in Colossians 2:6? It's a simple teaching that is difficult to live by.

_____

_____

_____

_____

In whom should we be "rooted" (2:7)? How can we be "built up"? What are some of the implications of being "rooted" and "built up"?

_____

_____

_____

_____

What are some practical ways you can open yourself up to letting God work in you?

_____

_____

_____

_____

How can we be "established in the faith" (2:7)? The idea here is not indoctrination, but following Christ with the support of other believers.

_____

_____

_____

_____

Do you "abound in thanksgiving" (2:7)? Being thankful is the cure to many of the problems that ail us. If you don't believe this, try it this week. Say thanks every morning for the breath in your lungs. Throughout each day this week look for things to be thankful for, and then thank God for them. Watch how your attitude will change. For what, and who, can you be thankful? Write down ten things you are thankful for, and then thank God for them in prayer.

_____

_____

_____

_____

CONCLUSION

Paul's stance toward suffering is ironic, yet unique. He sees suffering as an opportunity and an obligation. It gives him an opportunity to "fill up" the church. He is obligated, though, to use it as a means for revealing Christ's strength. When Paul became like Jesus, he was empowered.

Our lives change when we start viewing pain as an opportunity to show others who God is, and when our struggles become a way for Christ to show His strength. When we try to be like Jesus, we think, feel, and act differently. It's not easy letting Christ work through you, but it's transforming.

May you be empowered by Jesus, rooted in God and built up by other believers. May the Spirit work in you.

COLOSSIANS 2:8–23

We often treat the good news of Jesus like leftovers. We take what we learn in church, put it in Tupperware, and place it on a shelf. We access it when we're spiritually hungry, but ignore it otherwise. If we *only* eat when we have a spiritual nutritional need, we miss the colossal implications of Jesus' work; we miss the opportunity to be spiritually resurrected with Him.

Christ should be the center of everything we do. To make Christ the center, we have to understand His role in the physical and spiritual realm. According to Paul, powers we don't perceive are working to take our minds captive. By actively seeking Christ, they can be conquered. In the next eight studies of Colossians, we will open up the gospel and learn to let Christ reign in our lives.

ELEMENTAL SPIRITS AND CHRIST

Pray that Jesus would help you free your mind from false principles.

Read all of Colossians aloud in one sitting. Reflect on verse 2:8.

The verb Paul uses for "captive" (συλαγωγέω, *sulagōgeō*) has war connotations. He's saying we can be taken like bounty in a war. Why would he choose this term? How severe is his warning?

_____

_____

_____

_____

What can we be taken captive by? What type of "tradition" does Paul have in mind?

_____

_____

_____

_____

In what way can we be taken captive ("according to" what)?

_____

_____

_____

_____

The phrase "elemental spirits" (στοιχεῖα, *stoicheia*) could refer to spiritual beings, but it could also refer to a set of philosophical principles. Paul certainly was arguing against "human tradition" as a way to worship Jesus, but he could have also been saying that human tradition is used by spiritual beings to lead people astray. (The philosophy Paul had in mind was likely stoicism, which proposed that following a set of principles was the way to be enlightened by the gods.) Today, what ideas lead people astray? What false beliefs or religious traps do you find yourself falling into?

DEITY IN FLESH

Pray that God would help you overcome conscious and unconscious fears.

Read Colossians 1:1–2:23 aloud. Reflect on verses 2:9–10.

What does it mean for the "fullness of deity" to dwell in Christ's body (2:9)?

_____

_____

_____

_____

What is the significance of what God has accomplished in His Son?

_____

_____

_____

_____

How are we "filled" (2:10)? When Paul says "you have been filled," he is saying that Christ's work happened in the past—it is complete. But Paul also has present results in mind: Christ's work is continuing to happen—he is still filling us up, making us complete every day. Think about the connection between us "being filled" and "the fullness of deity" that dwelled in Christ (2:9). What are the implications of this connection for our lives?

_____

_____

_____

_____

By extension of what God has done in His Son, the Son is the "head of all rule and authority"—meaning that ultimately He has power over everything: all people, all things and all of creation. What authorities or powers do you fear? How can Christ help you overcome your fears? One of the keys to worshipping God with our entire being is overcoming our fears with His help.

_____

_____

_____

_____

CIRCUMCISION, BAPTISM AND RESURRECTION

 Pray the Spirit would reveal to you what it means to be resurrected with Christ.

 Read Colossians 1:24–2:23 aloud. Reflect on verses 2:11–12.

Paul uses the analogy of circumcision to describe the transformative work Christ has done in our lives. Circumcision was a symbol of God's covenant (His contract) with His people (Gen 17:15–27). But unlike physical circumcision, Christ's work is "made without hands" (Col 2:11). Paul follows with the phrase: "putting off the body of the flesh"—meaning to deny rituals, like circumcision, that are no longer required for God's family (2:8). Instead, we should affirm Christ's work in our lives. Paul then takes this analogy one step further to baptism (2:12). Circumcision and baptism both have to do with becoming part of God's family.

Paul says that we have been "buried" and "raised with Christ" (2:12). What he means is:

1. Our sins died with Christ on the cross—our debts were paid.

2. Our sins were left in the tomb with Christ when we chose to believe in Him—we don't have to suffer the consequences of them

3. We rose with Christ as new creations—meaning we can have a new, guilt-free life in relationship with God.

What is the "powerful working of God" (2:12)? How can the powerful working of God be more relevant in your life?

_____

_____

_____

_____

We have to make ourselves available for Christ's work. In order for us to be "raised with Christ," we have to hand over our lives to God for Him to control; we have to believe. What areas of your life do you need to hand over to God? If you just ask Him, He will work in you—He will change you.

_____

_____

_____

_____

ALIVE IN CHRIST

Pray that the Spirit would help you find freedom in Christ.

Read Colossians 2:6–2:23 aloud. Reflect on Colossians 2:13–15.

In what ways were we "dead" in our "trespasses and the uncircumcision" of our "flesh" (2:13)? (Think about what we learned in our study of Col 2:11–12.)

_____

_____

_____

_____

What did God do for us (2:13)? How does He bring change in our lives (2:14)?

_____

_____

_____

_____

If we die with Christ, we also rise with Christ (2:11–14). What are the implications of "all our trespasses" being "forgiven" (2:13–14)? What should our reaction be to what God has done through Christ?

_____

_____

_____

_____

When Paul speaks of the "the record of debt that stood against us" and "its legal demands," he's speaking about the implications of not following God's will—according to books like Exodus, Numbers, Leviticus and Deuteronomy. What did God do with these legal demands through Christ (2:14)?

_____

_____

_____

_____

Ultimately, what does Christ's sacrifice accomplish—both on the large scale and in each of our lives (2:15)?

_____

_____

_____

_____

What laws, ideas and notions are keeping you from accepting Christ's work? What is holding you back from fully embracing Jesus in all parts of your life?

_____

_____

_____

_____

QUALITY, NOT QUANTITY

Pray that the Spirit would help you release your religious notions about God and church.

Read Colossians 2:16–2:23 aloud. Reflect on verses 2:16–17.

We often measure our Christian success by our involvement in church. Although involvement in church is a must—for accountability and being used by Christ for the greater good—what *we do* is not what defines our relationship with God. Our relationship with God is defined by what *Christ has done* on our behalf. Our churches are imperfect because flawed people like us are involved. Nonetheless, when our churches care for other people, we get a small glimpse into God's ultimate goodness, love and mercy. In Colossians 2:16, Paul lists three things that were obstacles to believers in his day. He insists that people not be judged on the basis of flawed religious practices. What religious practices do you use to pass judgment on others?

_____

_____

_____

_____

What are the religious systems of Paul's day a "shadow of" (2:17)? What are the "things to come"? What "substance" is Paul saying "belongs to Christ"?

_____

_____

_____

_____

_____

The substance of what we do in church needs to be centered on the personhood and work of Christ. How can you better center your personal ministry on Jesus?

_____

_____

_____

_____

What needs to change about the way you approach church? What needs to change about the way you measure the quality of your relationship with Christ?

_____

_____

_____

_____

GROWTH DEFINED

🤚 *Pray that God would help you align your ideas about worship and growth with His own.*

📄 *Read Colossians 2:16–2:23 aloud. Reflect on verses 2:18–19.*

Some people use direct revelations from God (whether real or fictional) to make others feel like they have a lesser relationship with Him. Even though Paul himself had had an experience of Christ that transformed his life, he insists that such experiences should not lead to worship of other beings besides God, and not to worship practices that focus on us, instead of God ("asceticism") (2:18). What is dangerous about those who go on "in detail about visions" (2:18)?

_____

_____

_____

Why would someone from Paul's era "worship angels" (2:18)? What are people prone to worship today—in any world culture?

_____

_____

_____

How can you avoid being led astray by misinformed teaching or misdirected worship?

_____

_____

_____

To what should we "hold fast"? How is the church, "the body," held together?

_____

_____

_____

From whom should our growth as churches and as individuals come (2:19)? In what ways do you misrepresent (or misidentify) your personal growth or your church's growth? What changes do you need to make and how can you make these changes?

_____

_____

_____

RELIGION KILLS— JESUS SAVES

🤚 *Pray that the Spirit would help you identify the weak portions of your relationship with Jesus.*

📄 *Read Colossians 2:8-2:23 aloud. Reflect on verses 2:20-23.*

What things "perish as they are used" (2:20-22)? Who creates religious regulations (2:22)?

_____

_____

_____

_____

What appearances do religious regulations have (2:23)? When facades are stripped away, what are religious regulations, really (2:23)?

_____

_____

_____

What do "self-made religion" and "self-focused" religion (asceticism) do to the church, the body (2:23)? What does religion *not* do for us (2:23)?

_____

_____

_____

_____

We often confuse religion with Christianity. Likewise, we often confuse spirituality with Christianity. Religion leads us to believe that if we do what our church requires of us, we will be more holy and righteous. In the process, we can become dogmatic, hypocritical and judgmental. At times, we also believe that if we just focus on our devotional time, or community service projects, that God will think more highly of us. Doing more doesn't make us more valuable to God. We are all equal—sinners in need of grace. No matter what we do, we can't be good enough to earn God's grace. We need the death and resurrection of His Son to receive it. In return, we're called to strip ourselves of religiosity and self-focused spirituality. We are called to arm ourselves with an authentic and honest relationship with Jesus. That's the only way we can be like Him.

_____

_____

_____

_____

What side of the spectrum are you struggling with: religiosity or self-focused spirituality? How can God transform this part of your life?

_____

_____

_____

_____

RESURRECTED WITH CHRIST

Pray that the Spirit would help you to fully embrace Christ as He resurrects your life.

Read Colossians 1:1–3:1 aloud. Reflect on the first two chapters of the book.

Think about chapters 1 and 2 in light of 3:1: "If then you have been raised with Christ, seek the things that are above, where Christ is, seated at the right hand of God."

Take the time you would usually spend studying Colossians to think and pray about how Christ desires to "raise" you out of all of your struggles—all the things that bring spiritual death into your life.

Christ resurrecting us involves Him doing more than just saving us from our sins; He forgives us for each day. He also helps us when we need Him. In this regard, He can resurrect any part of our lives. Make a list of the top five things that you tend to place above Christ. Think about this in terms of what you spend time on or things you worry about. Next to each item, write down how you can place Christ above them. Ask someone to pray about these things with you, and continue to pray for you.

_____

_____

_____

How can you be resurrected with Christ each day? What areas of your life are still in need of resurrection?

_____

_____

_____

How can you bless other people with what Christ has done (and will do) in your life?

_____

_____

_____

_____

CONCLUSION

When we lean on our own abilities, we're doing what comes naturally. When we depend on Christ, we're doing something empowered by the supernatural—the work of God on earth.

If we fully embrace Jesus, He will resurrect our religious and self-dependent lives. He will make changes from within the body, the church. He will make all of us new, like the spiritually renewed body He possessed after rising from the dead.

May you embrace Christ's work and recognize that your sins and need for religion died on the cross. May you live a new, resurrected life empowered by Christ's miraculous resurrection, and use that life to bless other people.

COLOSSIANS 3:1–4:1

You may have heard Christianity is ethics supplemented with belief in Jesus. It's not, though. New Testament Christianity is radical. It forces us to ask: What kind of radicals will we be?

Jesus wanted to revolutionize the way people thought, acted and lived. The choice to believe in Jesus is step one. The choice to live ethically is a natural step two. But the choice to have your entire life shaped and defined by Jesus living vicariously through you—that is a difficult one. Christ in us, resurrecting us, has become uncommon theology. Yet that's what Paul preached.

There's a reason relationships of all kinds perplex us. There's a reason why ethical and moral dilemmas of everyday life defeat us. It's because we don't acknowledge that Jesus can, and desires to be, involved in every part of our lives. And in not acknowledging His power, we ignore the greatest part of Christianity: Christ wants to change our world through us.

In these next eight studies, Paul offers us practical tips for being like Jesus and explains how Christ can dwell in each of us and in our communities.

RAISED WITH CHRIST

Pray that God would help you seek things that are from above.

Read all of Colossians aloud in one sitting. Reflect on verses 3:1-4.

What does Paul tell us to seek (Col 3:1)?

_____

_____

_____

_____

Paul says Christ is "seated at the right hand of God" (3:1). To understand what this phrase means, run a search for "right hand" using Bible software or Biblia.com. Specifically look at how it is used in Exodus and the Psalms.

What is the difference between things "on earth" and "things that are above" (3:2)?

_____

_____

_____

_____

Where is your life "hidden" (3:3)? How is it hidden?

_____

_____

_____

When will Christ appear (3:4)? This passage has been connected with Christ's second coming, but considering that Paul doesn't talk about Christ's return anywhere else in Colossians, this interpretation seems unlikely. Instead, it seems Paul is talking about Christ appearing in our lives when we live like Him through the power of the Holy Spirit. Paul is essentially saying, "Jesus is here with us, among us, and working through us—now." And of course, we know, Christ is coming to earth again. How can you help make Christ apparent? Does Christ appear in your daily life?

WHY CHRIST DIED

Pray that the Spirit would help you overcome the sin in your life.

Read Colossians 1:1–4:1 aloud. Reflect on verses 3:5–10.

What should we "put to death" (3:5)? Jesus didn't die so that we could go on sinning; Jesus died so we could be sinless. We all know what sins we struggle with, even if we have a hard time admitting them to ourselves, but we have to openly confess our sins to overcome them. Tell Christ what you struggle with. Tell a friend. Tell your spouse. (Accountability works.) And then let the Spirit work in you to free you of your sin.

_____

_____

_____

_____

The wrath of God is coming (3:6), but not to those who trust Christ. That, though, is not the only reason Christ has given us eternal life (John 3:16–17). Christ resurrected us so that He could restore His earth by bringing heaven to it.

In what did we once walk (Col 3:7)? What should we "put away" (3:8)?

_____

_____

_____

_____

With whom do we need to be honest (3:9)? Are you living honestly and openly?

_____

_____

_____

_____

What should define your "new self" (3:10)? How can you be renewed?

_____

_____

_____

_____

GREEK, JEW, SLAVE, FREE—WHATEVER

Pray that Christ would help you to see past the differences between you and others.

Read Colossians 2:8–4:1. Reflect on verses 3:11–13.

To "put on a new self" via Christ (3:10) and be resurrected with Him (3:1) has implications not only for our personal lives, but also for our public lives. What divides us even though we are in Christ (3:11)? What did Paul want Christians of his day to do about cultural and racial divisions?

_____

_____

_____

_____

How does culture, specifically popular media, divide people today? Do you label people and categorize them?

_____

_____

_____

What would Paul say about labels and categorization? Remember labels run deep—even to subconscious levels. What should we "put on" (3:12)?

_____

_____

_____

How can you become better at "bearing with" others and forgiving others (3:13)? Why should you forgive? Whom do you need to forgive?

_____

_____

_____

_____

IT'S NOT NEW-AGE CHRISTIANITY—JUST PAUL'S CHRISTIANITY

 *Pray that God would help you to love more graciously.*

Read Colossians 2:16–3:17. Reflect on verses 3:14–15.

When the Beatles sang "all you need is love," they were articulating a view of their generation. The idea wasn't new. When people categorized as new-agers say, "just love," they're also not saying anything new. Unfortunately, this truth is not always lived out the way God intended. Love isn't all we need; we also need truth. Paul said "put on love" because "it binds everything together in perfect harmony" (Col 3:14). Paul understood that Christ-like love will keep us from sinning and help us live righteously, for the betterment of others. The best way to get over yourself is to start living for the good of someone else. Doing something helpful for someone else helps you put your problems in perspective—this is Paul's Christianity.

What is Paul's advice for being like Jesus (3:14)? How does he categorize Christ-like action?

_____

_____

What should rule our hearts (3:15)? What were we called to do? (When Paul refers to "one body," he is talking about the Church—those who gather in Christ's name.)

_____

_____

_____

Letting Christ rule means framing our desires and actions with Him in mind. What areas of your public life are not ruled by Christ?

_____

_____

_____

To whom specifically can you show more love? How can you show more love to people each and every day?

_____

_____

_____

CHRIST DWELLS IN US

Pray that the Spirit would help you embrace the idea of Christ living vicariously through you.

Read Colossians 3:1–3:17. Reflect on verses 3:16–17.

Why should we let the "word of Christ dwell in [us] richly" (3:16)?

_____

_____

_____

_____

Bible study is not merely an intellectual exercise; it's also a spiritual exercise. It prepares us for the future and helps us handle what is happening now. What should we do with the word of Christ? How can we act upon the word of Christ (3:16)? What mediums can we use?

_____

_____

_____

_____

What should we do "in the name of the Lord Jesus" (3:17)? Why should we be thankful (3:15, 17)?

_____

_____

_____

_____

Being thankful to God requires prayer. It's a mindset for approaching life and an acknowledgement that all that we have comes from Him. It's an internal guidance system. What is your mindset? How does it need to change?

_____

_____

_____

_____

PAUL REDEFINES CULTURE

🤚 *Pray that Christ would help you be Christ-like in how you approach all of your relationships.*

📑 *Read Colossians 3:12–4:1. Reflect on verses 3:18–19.*

Colossians 3:18–19 is often taken out of context. Ignore the section heading in your Bible above 3:18 and the chapter break at 4:1. This will help you recognize how 3:18–4:1 is connected to 3:12–17. What does a wife submitting to her husband have to do with thankfulness?

_____

_____

_____

_____

What does a husband loving his wife, and not being harsh, have to do with thankfulness (3:19)?

_____

_____

_____

In Paul's time, a wife being forced to submit to her harsh husband was probably common. We know this because of Roman law. Paul's command to wives was contingent upon husbands not being harsh. No one should endure an abusive relationship of any kind. Paul's command does not offer husbands the right to be domineering or to have the final say. It's the opposite: it's a call to leadership, mutual respect and love. Also remember that Paul is addressing Christians who are meant to live by the principles he lays out in 3:1–12. In this regard, Paul's view on women was revolutionary.

What would Paul say if he addressed Christians today? Is 3:18–19 still relevant today? Consider this verse in light of relationships in general, not just marriage.

_____

_____

_____

_____

What types of people should you submit to and obey?

_____

_____

_____

Ultimately, to whom should we all submit ourselves? What does Jesus want each of us to do in all of our relationships?

_____

_____

_____

How is thankfulness connected to our view of relationships?

_____

_____

_____

THE KIDS AREN'T ALRIGHT

Pray that God would help you show Christ's love to your family.

Read Colossians 3:12–4:1. Reflect on verses 3:20–21.

When should children obey their parents (3:20)? Why does it "please God" for children to obey their parents? Does this verse apply in all situations? Think about it in light of what we learned in Lesson 38 about the way Christians are called to treat their spouses and people in general.

_____

_____

_____

What does Paul mean when he says, "do not provoke your children" (3:21)? Why does Paul single out fathers (3:21)? Could this be another example of Paul redefining a first-century concept? (Also think about this question in light of what we learned previously.)

_____

_____

_____

Read Luke 18:15–17. How did Jesus approach children?

_____

_____

_____

What would Paul say if he addressed Christians today? Is Colossians 3:20–21 still relevant today?

_____

_____

_____

What does God want to teach you about the children in your family and the other children you know? We often forget that we were once children.

_____

_____

_____

DID PAUL SUPPORT SLAVERY?

Pray that Jesus would teach you how to live like Him—no matter what your situation is.

Read Colossians 3:1–4:1. Reflect on verses 3:22–4:1.

Just like the other relationships Paul mentions, slavery is still a real problem in the world. Some people have taken Paul's advice about slaves in 3:22–4:1 to be implicit acceptance of slavery. This is not the case. Paul is offering advice for dealing with a system. Paul makes this clear when he says there is neither slave nor free person (3:10). He also makes this clear in the book of Philemon, a letter which was brought to a leader of the church in Colossae.

Furthermore, not all slavery in Paul's day was evil and corrupt; some of it involved working off a debt. It was a form of legitimate labor, similar to how we pay off credit cards—the only difference being that we don't work directly for the lender. In this regard, Paul is also talking about general work in 3:22–4:1. And work is something nearly all of us do. How did Paul suggest slaves obey (3:22)? Is this applicable to your job?

_____

_____

_____

_____

Who are you serving when you work (3:23–24)? What do you receive when you work (3:24)?

_____

_____

_____

_____

How is justice delivered to those who treat people wrongly and those who steal (3:25)?

_____

_____

_____

How did Paul suggest masters treat their slaves, and why did he suggest this (4:1)?

_____

_____

_____

What would Paul say if he addressed Christians today? Is 3:22–4:1 still relevant today? What does God want to teach us about how we work, how we treat others. For whom do we work?

_____

_____

_____

CONCLUSION

Paul is pragmatic. His pragmatism, though, is always rooted in a theological reality: the life-altering work of Christ. Christ desires to be involved in everything we do. Involving Him can change the dynamics of relationships and make the solution for ethical dilemmas clear.

May you embrace Christ's revolutionary work. May God resurrect you with Christ and Christ give you a new life. May His spirit work through you to change the world.

COLOSSIANS 4:2–18

The gospel seems simple; wherever God will lead us looks normal. Yet, Paul calls Christ a mystery—a mystery for which Paul was imprisoned (4:3). We should be constantly trying to make sense of that mystery.

Paul believed in his cause all the more fervently because of his imprisonment. He's not the only person to have done this: Martin Luther King, Jr. comes to mind, as do Peter and Justin the Martyr. We often can't grasp where or how they found courage. The most profound thing isn't what they did, but their audacity to go on. What makes something worth wearing chains that rub your skin raw? What makes something worth death? Only one thing: something beyond the temporal. Eternity is worth chains and death—as is the hope of other people having eternal life.

Most of us only have small glimpses into what Paul's lot was like. Few of us have ever been beaten physically for Jesus, but we have all been beaten spiritually. These moments give us a chance to witness the mystery of Christ. Saying we are open to experiencing Christ's mystery is easier than living it. The moment we truly embrace the work of Jesus, we start to see things we don't expect and often don't desire.

For most of us, life with Jesus is "normal" because we haven't seen how amazing the "abnormal" life with Him can be. In the next eight studies, you will see why Paul was willing to give everything for Christ. You will learn that you have an opportunity to do the same.

WHY WE PRAY

🤚 *Pray that God would help you be thankful and watchful.*

📄 *Read all of Colossians aloud in one sitting. Reflect on verse 4:2.*

Thankfulness and watchfulness are such profound concepts that they are worth considering for a whole week—really for a whole lifetime. This isn't an exaggeration. Paul places the idea of being thankful and watchful within the framework of prayer. How can we apply these concepts to our prayer life?

_____

_____

_____

_____

Look up "thankfulness" in a concordance, search for it using Biblia.com, or use Bible software. In what contexts is it used? (Examining the way that Paul and other New Testament writers used the term will help to perceive the ideas he was evoking.) Look specifically at Philippians 4.

This is the third time Paul has mentioned being thankful in Colossians. What do Colossians 1:3 and 3:15 tell us about Paul's view of thankfulness? When is he thankful? Why is he thankful? Keep in mind that he was in a Roman prison— likely in a pit and chained to a Roman guard—because of his belief in Christ.

_____

_____

_____

_____

_____

"Being watchful" means being attentive, even perceptive. It doesn't mean worrying. Search for "watchful" using Biblia.com or Bible software. In what contexts is it used? Specifically examine Galatians 5–6. For what should you keep watch?

Name four things for which you need to be thankful. Name three things you should watch for. If you did these things, how would your life be different? Try doing being thankful and watchful for one week, and see what habits you develop.

WHAT WE USUALLY DON'T PRAY FOR

Pray that the Spirit would help you perceive what you should be praying for.

Read Colossians 1:1–4:4 aloud in one sitting. Reflect on verses 4:3–4.

For what should we be praying (4:3)? Who opens doors (4:3)?

_____

_____

_____

_____

Why would Paul choose the term "mystery" to describe Christ (4:3)? Think about this question in light of Paul's imprisonment and suffering. Paul also discusses mystery in Colossians 1:26 and 2:2. What do these passages tell us about his view of mystery? (Also see Eph 1:9, 3:3, 5:32 and 6:19.)

_____

_____

_____

_____

Why was the "mystery of Christ" such an important concept to Paul? What did it prompt him to do and help him understand?

_____

_____

_____

For what does Paul need clarity (4:4)? Do you need clarity? Like Paul, you could ask other people to pray about matters that are unclear.

_____

_____

_____

How can you experience the mystery of Christ more often? If you did so, what would change about your current circumstances?

_____

_____

_____

OUTSIDERS EATING YOUR TABLE SALT

🤚 *Pray that Christ would grant you wisdom when you discuss your faith with others.*

📄 *Read Colossians 2:8–4:6. Reflect on verses 4:5–6.*

Read Mark 4:11. Who are the outsiders Paul is referencing in Colossians 4:5? Why do we need "wisdom toward outsiders" (4:5)? The concepts of discernment and wisdom are closely connected.

_____

_____

_____

Carpe diem, meaning "seize the day," isn't only a Latin sentiment. Paul tells us to make the best use of our time (4:5). He is referencing how we spend our time with people who don't believe in Jesus ("outsiders" to the faith). In light of this, what should our relationships with people who don't believe in Jesus look like?

_____

_____

_____

How should we speak to other people (4:6)? How can we be gracious with other people?

_____

_____

_____

Read Mark 9:50. What does it mean to season our relationships with salt? How will seasoning our relationships help us answer each person (Col 4:6)? What happens when salt is missing?

_____

_____

_____

Which of your current relationships need more salt? How can you bring salt to them?

_____

_____

_____

BEING LIKE JESUS MEANS BEING A GOOD FRIEND

Pray that God would show you how you can better the lives of others.

Read Colossians 2:16–4:18. Reflect on verses 4:7–9.

It's always difficult to part with those we love, even if we know that they need to bless someone else. Knowing that doesn't change the way we feel about them or help us stop missing them. Paul repeatedly parted ways with key ministry partners and friends. In doing so, he set an example for us. When the people we love are needed somewhere else, we need to give them a splendid send-off.

_____

_____

_____

When was the last time someone called you a "dear friend"? If it wasn't recent, invest more in your friendships. How can you, like Tychicus, be someone's close friend ("beloved brother"), "faithful servant" and "fellow slave" (4:7)?

_____

_____

_____

If you were loyal like Paul, what would your relationships look like? Imagine the lives that could be transformed. What changes do you need to make to live more like Tychicus?

_____

_____

_____

How can you, like Tychicus, encourage the hearts of other people (4:8)?

_____

_____

_____

What makes someone "faithful and beloved" like Onesimus (4:9)? For the context of Paul's reference to Onesimus, read the book of Philemon. (It's one of the shortest books in the New Testament; it won't take long.) What turns someone from a runaway into a faithful and beloved friend?

_____

_____

_____

Paul wants his followers to tell other churches "everything that has taken place" in his recent ministry (4:9). Are you proud enough of your circumstances to have someone tell all the details of them? If not, what needs to change so you can be?

_____

_____

_____

WORKING FOR THE MAN

Pray that the Spirit would reveal God's calling upon your life, and help you pursue that calling.

Read Colossians 3:1–4:18. Reflect on verses 4:10–11.

Paul was not alone in prison. Who was with him (4:10)? Why does Paul send instructions about his friends (4:7-9)?

_____

_____

_____

Do you regularly recommend friends to other people? If not, it's a good habit to pick up. When we positively recommend other people—who deserve the recommendation, of course—we build relationships. We need to work together as friends, colleagues, ministries and companies. Together, we can accomplish more. Paul's model worked—just look at how many churches there are around the world today. He created a legacy that far surpassed him and his lifetime. He did so by investing in people: caring for them and loving them, then sending them out to help other people. He gave other people his investments.

By "men of the circumcision," Paul means fellow Jews (4:11). Paul was working with people like him and unlike him. He crossed racial boundaries to further the gospel. Paul was convinced to do so by his boss. For whom did Paul work? What was the purpose of his ministry?

_____

_____

_____

_____

Does your purpose align with Paul's? If your purpose does not align with his, are you out of line with God's purpose?

_____

_____

_____

Keep in mind that Paul had a day job—tent-making. This didn't stop him from being one of the most effective ministers of all time. What is God calling you to do? If you aren't following God's calling, why aren't you?

_____

_____

_____

What steps do you need to take to do more of God's work?

_____

_____

_____

PROMOTING OTHERS WILL CHANGE YOU

Pray that the Spirit would reveal whom you should be promoting and giving credit to.

Read Colossians 3:5–4:18. Reflect on verses 4:12–14.

When Paul says that "Epaphras … is one of you," he likely means that Epaphras is from the Colossae church. Paul says that Epaphras is "a servant of Christ Jesus" (4:12). The word for "servant" here literally means "slave." Epaphras was enslaved to the mission of Christ. This was the commitment level required of Christians in the first century. Without that commitment level, someone would not be able to endure the persecution that came with being like Jesus.

How does Paul describe Epaphras' prayers (4:12)? Why does Paul place such an emphasis on prayer? (Think about this question in light of the second half of 4:12.)

_____

_____

_____

_____

Why do we usually recommend people? Contrast this with how—and why— Paul recommends people (4:12-13). What does this tell you about what it means to be a Christian?

_____

_____

_____

_____

Paul also sends his greetings from other believers. How often do you tie your ministry work with the work of others? To whom should you be giving credit?

_____

_____

_____

SPREADING THE WORD ISN'T A NEW IDEA

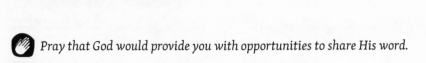

Pray that God would provide you with opportunities to share His word.

Read Colossians 4:1–4:12. Reflect on verses 4:15–17.

The Colossians were instructed to pass on this letter to the church (or churches) at Laodicea, and to give their greetings to a church ran by a woman named Nympha (4:15–16). Likewise, Paul wrote another letter to the Laodiceans that was intended to be shared with the Colossians (4:16). Pass the letter of Colossians on to someone else, like the Colossians did. Share it on Facebook or Twitter. Email it to a friend. Navigate to Colossians on Biblia.com and click "Share." You can even try reading all of Colossians aloud to someone who you usually wouldn't study the Bible with.

We often think that *we* have to do all of God's work, but His Word does more than we could ever imagine. All we have to do is be willing to share it. Most people have never read the entire Bible, so chances are it will be new and interesting to them, depending on where they are in their relationship with God.

The words that Paul tells the Colossians to pass on to Archippus are powerful: "See that you fulfill the ministry that you have received in the Lord" (4:17). What ministry does God want you to fulfill? What ministry have you received?

_____

_____

_____

_____

_____

What does God want you to do? Are you doing it? If you're not, how can you start doing it? If you are, how can you be more effective in your ministry?

_____

_____

_____

REMEMBER

Pray for those suffering for Jesus—remember them.

Read all of Colossians aloud in one sitting, as Paul instructs in 4:16. Reflect on verse 4:18.

Paul ends his letter by writing a greeting with his own hand. In the first century, letters were written by professional scribes. Paul writes this last greeting with his own hand to prove that this letter comes from him. (Pseudonymous letters were common.) Paul's penmanship would have been distinct from the professional scribe.

What does Paul request that the church remember (4:18)? There is power in remembrance. That's why we have moments of silence and days of remembrance. The collective memory of a community can change the world.

_____

_____

_____

_____

_____

Does your community remember those suffering for Jesus? Do you care for them and support them? If not, how can you do so?

_____

_____

_____

_____

_____

Paul closes his letter by saying, "Grace to you." He wishes grace upon the believers. Do you wish grace upon other people? If you were more gracious, would your life change? Would you be more appreciated if you were more gracious? Grace is reciprocal.

_____

_____

_____

_____

CONCLUSION

Central to Colossians is the idea that Christ is meant to be at the center of our lives. For Paul, Jesus is not just the center of his universe, but of the entire universe. He was there in the beginning of creation, and continues to be at the center of all things. Putting Christ first is an acknowledgment of the natural order of things. The conviction that Jesus drives everything in our lives seems abnormal to most people, yet it is God's norm.

If we as Christians really are abnormal compared to everyone else, we will probably suffer for Jesus, just like Paul did. Suffering is a product of the human and spiritual powers that oppose Jesus—the resistance to God's reign. The mystery of Christ is meant to transform our reality. Some people and spiritual beings don't want that transformation to happen, so chaos in our lives will ensue at times. Our arsenal against this is thankfulness, watchfulness, prayer and grace.

We're not meant to accept Jesus and then live like everyone else. We're meant to live differently, to remember those who suffer, and to be the godly seasoning in the lives of everyone around us.

God wants you to be a new creation, and He wants to create good things through you. May you be like Jesus. Make Him central in your life, then watch everything around you transform.

Make Your Bible Study Even Better

Get 30% off Bible Study Magazine.

Subscribe today!

BibleStudyMagazine.com/Subscribe

1-800-875-6467 or +1-360-527-1700 (Int'l)